A

REDEFINED

WOMAN

*Living Life with
Higher Definition*

by Rebecca St.Louis

ISBN-13: 978-0-578-80999-1

Cover design by Jeremy Williams
Edited by Micaelle E. Previl
Printed in the United States of America

This book is dedicated to:

My little angel MJ.

You are the light of my life.

Table of Contents

Preface

*Your life has a high definition,
a higher purpose with
a higher meaning.*

here is a pivotal moment in every woman's life. It's that sudden moment when you are ready for change. The moment where the fulfillment of life, destiny, and purpose come into alignment. It is the moment when your purpose is rumbling from the depths of your soul. Destiny overtakes your mind, and faith is pressed upon your heart. Indeed, it is a significant moment where creative capabilities and possibilities are insurmountable.

This moment, my friends, is called your defining moment. It's when *Chronos* (the Greek word for "time") becomes valid, and the paradigm shift *Kairos* (the Greek word for "appointed time or opportune moment") comes into fruition. Although *Chronos* and *Kairos* both deal with timing, they are actually different.

The defining moment I am speaking of coincides with *Kairos*. *Kairos* is that defining hour and season where momentum is at an all-time speed. It's when the winds of change are blown to accelerate a new blessing. I've come to announce that your *Kairos* moment is here. Your moment of favor has arrived. You are presently experiencing the perfect occasion to thrive and live in a new perspective concerning your purpose. A wind of change has blown in your direction, and that means that your season has emerged.

Now is the right time to come into a new realization. Real things happen for real people, and the reality is, your life has meaning. Yet, in addition to that realization beloved, you must understand that you can bring new significance to your life.

The purpose of this book is to assist you as you work to redefine yourself in its entirety. I'm writing to you, dear sister (and dear brother), so that you can tap into the force that has been with you all along. I want to welcome you to the life that has always been yours. Eons ago, televisions needed antennas and perhaps the help of a hanger to acquire a clear picture. Today my dears, TVs have evolved to where they now possess high definition.

I want you to know that your life also has a high definition, a higher purpose with a higher meaning. Redefinition concerns providing something with a new meaning. Jesus Christ came to Earth so that our lives would have a new significance. He confirms this in Jn. 10:10, where He says, "The thief does not come except to steal, and to kill, and to destroy. I have come that they may have life, and that they may have it more abundantly" (NIV).

Christ came to give us a life of fullness, plentifulness, and fulfillment. Life from an eternal perspective is a life with high definition. A life full of illumination and clarity is what Christ intends for your life.

"His Story" being fulfilled through you is the high definition He wants to give you. I want to further discuss the benefits of Christ redefining your life. I hope that you will gain a deeper understanding as to why it's so imperative to be redefined. I want you to understand who you are and whose you are.

I believe you chose the right book. I want to share my thoughts with you, and enlighten your understanding with Godly wisdom and the word of God, so that you'll be well-equipped and informed of what God requires of you. It's time to see yourself with a higher view; it's time to see others from a different perspective: a kingdom perspective. Let's go deeper and make this moment matter. This is your moment to be changed and redefined. My dear friends, there's nothing blurry about your destiny. Your definition is so high and so clear. So, let's click on the remote of your life. It's time for a redefined motion picture. A redefining view. A redefined life.

Who We Are

> *To know where you're going,*
> *you've got to know who you are.*
> *Women are the crème de la crème,*
> *the icing to the cake. They are the*
> *seasoning God adds, which makes*
> *everything taste good. Women are*
> *gifted, and they are certainly*
> *needed. If no one ever told you that*
> *you mattered, Sister Girl, let me do*
> *it for you, one time. You. Matter.*

Women are revolutionary, remarkable, regal, righteous, radiant, radical, astounding, audacious, amazing, world-fighting, world-changing, warfare-waging warriors. Simply put, we are RAW: REAL ANOINTED WOMEN.

These are just a few words that exemplify the powerful virtuous woman. Over time, women have been the best second edition of man. They have cleaved to their men and supplied every need in their homes. Women have served, nurtured, given birth, and submissively yielded to the leadership of strong men. Whether playing the dual roles of mother and father (married or single), women are strong, whole, independent, vibrant, proactive, and intelligent creatures.

Women bring much-needed zest, and when we touch, we make things happen. From Eve, in the garden, to Commander/Judge Deborah, even to former First Lady Michelle Obama in the White House, women have rocked the ages with their power and strength.

As women of Zion who travail and reach higher heights, we have an original, yet individualistic imprint. We are crafted and made in the very image of God. Our stamp and signature cannot be duplicated or replicated. We are the jewels to every king's crown. The power invested in us isn't just human strength; it is divine, supernatural ability.

Women of faith are anointed to rule, legislate, and win battles victoriously. We are royal recipients of a kingly inheritance. Women are valuable, influential, and needed. We are relevant with time, raw and gifted with purpose. Women Rock! We are the soft breeze that blows on a sunny day. Women are the neck that holds the head, and we are the wow factor that is added to every man.

When a man finds a woman, he says, "Wow!" because he has seen his Eve (rib) for the first time. And when she is with him, everyone who sees her says, "Wow!" Her WOW factor or what makes her special is the fact that she's a woman of worship, a willing woman, and a woman who wars! Women are poised, modest, and classy. We are the essential ingredient that adds flavor and special touches to everything around us. The love we give, the help we bring, and the presence we carry make this world a better place. Most assuredly, women matter.

I can only speak from my view as to who we are, but the word of God shows us who and whose we are. My dear sisters, you need to understand that you are so important. I know someone in your past or present has said that you are worthless. I'm sure some guy has devalued you, and you feel like you don't measure up, especially based on society's standards. But, can I reveal something to you? You matter.

Nothing anyone says about you defines you. God has already defined you, and no matter what anyone says, you should know that people's words are just opinions. They're not facts. Who cares what people have said or done to you? What has happened to you didn't break who you are. Society's labels didn't cause your existence. God's word did. Everything you have faced up to now has shaped and molded your identity. Who you were is a person you'll never be again. The wounds, the scars, the emotional letdowns, and disappointments didn't break you. They helped to make you stronger.

No matter what anyone has told you, their opinions don't measure up to who God says you are. God has skillfully and wonderfully made you. You aren't weak, defeated, disfigured, ugly, or stupid. Sure, you've failed here or there. Maybe you experienced a few boo-boos and bumps along your way. Tell me who hasn't? Your mistakes don't change who you are — they represent the risks you were willing to take. They also exemplify the lessons you learned, that will enable you to make better choices in the future.

The definition of your life will never be found in the mouths of others. The meaning of your life can only be found in God's. In fact, the Lord adds His word to you every day. Daily. He defines you. The Bible says in Matt. 4:4, "But He answered and said, "It is written, "Man shall not live by bread alone, but by every word that proceeds from the mouth of God" (NKJV). That means that God spoke your existence, and His words live in you. You exist because God called you to life; what He has said and still says defines you.

All that your life entails only come through God's word over your life. Undoubtedly, His word hovers over and protects you. We develop and learn while we apply the knowledge of the word — this is how we grow in the Lord. While you grow with Him, you discover more about yourself. Once you acquire a deep under-standing of God's word, you will be able to acknowledge that you have been bought at a very high price.

No matter what has been spoken over our lives or who has hurt us, the word of God comes to fill us, change us, and conform us. We even overcome by the living word of God. That is why the words of the past cannot dictate your definition. Your life is a beautiful, authentic story. You are the result of God's creative miracle. You are His masterpiece, and He didn't make a mistake when He created you. You are the Lord's model on the earth. You are His royal gem. You rule with power and divinity. Virtue and power are inside of you. The scriptures tell us in 2 Cor. 4:7, "But we have this treasure in earthen vessels, that the excellency of the power may be of God, and not of us" (ISV).

You don't just hold treasures. You are an invaluable treasure that is far more precious than rubies. When God created mankind, He made an investment in us. He deposited His very likeness into us and gave us dominion, divine authority, skills, and strategy. In addition to strength, we were given the mandate to worship, honor God, and decree and declare what we desire to come into fruition.

You may ask, "Rebecca, what are you talking about?" I want you to understand that you've got the power, honey. God had a predestined image of who you are before you even realized who you were. You are precious, you are loved, and without you, there wouldn't be many others.

As you ponder on your flaws or slip-ups, take a moment and look at your beauty. What do you see? Does what you see about yourself define who you are? No. Your definition has already been given. The errors of your past have no hold on who you are about to become. You aren't a failure. You are worth every good thing life has to offer. You are so extraordinary and so very important that the greatest Hero of all time thought you were worth dying for.

You may say, "I'm not this or that," but God says you're more. He says you are worthy, wanted, loved, precious, powerful, beautiful, and so much more:

You are fearfully and wonderfully made.

I praise you because I am fearfully and wonderfully made; your works are wonderful, I know that full well.

Ps. 139:14 NIV

I have a plan for you.

For I know the plans I have for you," declares the Lord, "plans to prosper you and not to harm you, plans to give you hope and a future.

Jer. 29:11 NIV

You are a good thing.

He who finds a wife finds a good thing and obtains favor from the LORD.

Prov. 18:22 NASB

You are free in Christ.

It is for freedom that Christ has set us free. Stand firm, then, and do not let yourselves be burdened again by a yoke of slavery.

Gal. 5:1 NIV

You have been given every spiritual blessing in the heavenly places.

Praise be to the God and Father of our Lord Jesus Christ, who has blessed us in the heavenly realms with every spiritual blessing in Christ.

Eph. 1:3 NIV

You have been made complete in Christ.

And in Him you have been made complete [achieving spiritual stature through Christ], and He is the head over all rule and authority [of every angelic and earthly power].

Col. 2:10 AMP

These scriptures are just a few reminders of what the word says about you. You are who God says that you are. You've been redeemed by the Lord Jesus Christ. And I believe upon the completion of this book, your life will be repositioned, revived, and renewed. Now that you know who you are and whose you are, I want you to believe it. I want you to walk with your head up high and embrace that you are everything God says you are. Never forget that you are highly favored.

II

Virtuous? What's That?

"Virtuous? Oh, I've heard that word before. It means to be pure, right? No? Wait, does it mean I should be married? What does it mean to be virtuous?"

eing virtuous can mean for some, that they must live righteously, that women should live up to a certain standard. What does it mean to you? Why is it even necessary to discuss virtuosity?

According to Webster's dictionary, a virtuous person is righteous, ethical, and moral. A virtuous woman is considered to be honorable and upheld with the highest esteem. For some women, it's just a mere word that bears no meaning or value. Many, in fact, choose to exist in their ignorance. For many others, being a virtuous woman is THE goal.

As a young woman who grew up in a Christian household, I was taught to live with reverence for God and respect for others. I learned that I had to be modest and live a disciplined life.

I can honestly say that it wasn't easy. I was tempted, tested, and tried, and I felt like the standard set before me as a young Christian was impossible to attain. Now being virtuous wasn't just difficult. I didn't even know what it meant. I knew I had to learn, and it just seemed like too much work. And to be honest, I didn't see the point when my entire life, I felt like a failure.

I preferred living my own way, with my definition of who I was, entirely distorted by shame. I sincerely believed that I was a mess. I was comfortable procrastinating, highly insecure, and faithfully failing in many areas. I could never finish my tasks or assignments.

I desired relationships that carried no weight or value to my life. I always felt the need to fit in, and it was always with the wrong crowd. I wanted my light to be seen and my life to be bright, but I wanted the power to come through people. I eventually learned through my experiences that there was more in store for me. My life held weight on God's scale. I didn't know why or how, but I knew He gave me something, and it didn't belong to me. He gave me a life that I couldn't give myself. He woke me up every day by saying, "Live." Albeit, I had no clue how to do it. I felt stuck, so lost. I needed a touch. I needed God's guidance. Like Esther, I was put in a hard place. I had to make decisions fast. All of that led to a defining moment, where I no longer wanted to be lost, wandering in confusion. I had to take a risk and believe that God would lead me.

I had always wondered what type of woman I would become. Who would I be? What moral standards would I live by? What high level of influence would I operate under? What would I leave behind for other women to follow? For so many reasons, I was haunted by these questions, and I needed straightforward answers.

So I went to the only One who could provide them. I was desperate to have clarity, and over time, God gave it to me. I prayed, and I asked God to reveal to me who I was. As I sought Him, He showed me Proverbs 31 and helped me to see the identity and standard expected of every woman of faith.

In Proverbs 31, I found a full description of what being a virtuous woman entails. The scripture declares that the virtuous woman is a strong God-fearing, yielded vessel. She brings forth a blessing in her home. She submissively serves under the hardworking, Godly man. The virtuous woman is praised by her peers and honored by her husband. She invokes the very presence and increase of God's provision on behalf of her family. Her husband and her children call her blessed. She demands and legislates with her divine anointing and queenly authority. Her worth far exceeds that of the most precious jewels.

The virtuous woman is a worshiper. She's innovative, ambitious, and entrepreneurial. With her skillful nature and persuasive touch, she makes things happen. She's the bonding force and the matriarch.

Aiding and facilitating as the suitable helper, she sets the tone of every place she treads her feet upon. A woman filled with reverence, power, integrity, modesty, and grace: that is the virtuous woman. Oh, and for those of you who think you need to be a virgin or married to bear the name, you are sadly mistaken. A virtuous woman is a woman full of God's presence, power, and love. She's strong, whether she's single or not. She's already set apart.

She is filled with the Lord, remains in tune with Him, while staying focused and perfecting being a daughter, which materializes the wife she already is, for *the one* she awaits. She's basically what Eve was before the Fall in Eden. Truly, she is complete. Thanks be to Christ, who has made our hope in Him a reality we can achieve. As we strive to be like Him, and because we are His chosen people, our transformation from impurity to purity becomes sure.

Matt. 25:1-13 explains the story of the 10 virgins with their lamps. Five were foolish, and five that were wise. When the time came for the bridegroom to get them, the foolish were busy trying to buy extra oil because their lamps were empty. The wise, however, had enough oil because they were already prepared with more than enough.

Assuredly, wisdom will tell you to be prepared, and folly will make you complacent, thinking that having just enough is more than enough. As it says in Prov. 3:35, "The wise shall inherit glory (all honor and good), but shame is the highest rank conferred on self-confident fools" (AMP).

This parable is a depiction of how women can be. Some of us are not humble. We are self-reliant and independent. We aren't prepared for the arrival of our bridegroom (the Lord). We are comfortably content with enough. We've been accustomed to the ease of this carnal life. We don't prepare for the future. We don't want to work to be different. We want the easy way out. We don't want to store anything for later. We want what's right now.

A woman of God has enough wisdom to save for later. She has to be set apart and set a standard to be ready. The parable isn't only about being pure, it's also about being prepared as you maintain your purity. It concerns embracing the mentality of a virgin. It involves having a pure approach and consciousness. A life that's filled with real substance and oil. A full life that's overflowing with the depth of God's anointing and glory.

Simply put, the foolish virgins missed the mark. The wise virgins prepared for the coming of their one desire. Their groom. A lesson we can learn from this parable is that the grace of God follows the woman who chooses to walk readily. Grace accompanies you as you press toward the promise and purpose that's set before you (Phil. 3:14).

Five is the number of grace. The spiritual significance of this, as it relates to the parable, is that grace guided and governed the five wise virgins. And it is available to you now. Grace is here to keep you and to help you reach your goals. It has been freely given to help you develop your life totally: "But to each one of us grace has been given as Christ apportioned it" (Eph. 4:7, NIV).

Proverbs 31 is the model and example. However, Jesus Christ came to give you grace. It has been freely given so that this model can be your inspiration for His demonstration in you. He's given you a Helper, Comforter, and Guide through the Holy Spirit. Being a virgin at heart makes you different. It sets you apart and makes you a candidate to be chosen for the arrival of your Master. And so, virtuosity entails a pure life, seek, and approach. It is this virtuous anointing that sets you up for your pickup.

A man searching for a wife is looking for a ready wife. She is whole inside and out. She does not lack anything. I want you to know that the standard written in Proverbs 31 is obtainable. When a woman is positioned for a pickup, she comes ready at the moment of pickup. When we seek to be filled with God's virtue, we are filled with His power, and we possess His full essence inside of us.

You must keep in mind that the virtuous woman is not perfect. She doesn't dot every I or crosses every T. You may feel that your mistakes disqualify you. However, I'm here to tell you that being virtuous has nothing to do with just being physically pure. Virtuosity is a state of being. It concerns being one (in mind, body, soul, and spirit) with God. It's a wholeness of identity, purification of the heart rather than the flesh. I must emphasize that being redefined and virtuous is not about acting or showing that you are. It's about allowing God to be what He needs to be through you, for you, for His glory. It entails being able to accept the pure touch of God who will birth new things through you.

Just like the virgin, Mary (see Lk. 1-2). Mary wasn't just chosen because she was naturally a virgin. She also had the character and heart of a virgin: "And beside this, giving all diligence, add to your faith virtue; and to virtue knowledge" (2 Pet. 1:5 KJV).

In my own life, I struggled with allowing God's word to dress me. The words of my past and the things I had done had robbed me of believing that I could be virtuous. I allowed my fears and insecurities to stifle me from success. The thoughts of my mistakes made me feel unworthy.

I dated so many men and let the words of different relationships strip me of my identity. God's word was clear and written in all its power, but as I read Proverbs 31, I couldn't see how I could measure up to such a standard.

On a side note, you may also believe that renewal is impossible and that you shouldn't claim virtuosity as your identity. But I've come to denounce those lies from the pits of hell. In the name of Jesus, I rebuke guilt, condemnation, and false, futile thoughts that make you think you're unworthy. The blood of Jesus releases you today, from fear and the grips of condemnation. Rom. 8:1 says, "Therefore, there is now no condemnation for those who are in Christ Jesus." The moment you and I accepted Jesus, we became new.

However, let's come back to my story. I felt like I had failed God countlessly, and I was in denial about who I was because I knew He required more, but I didn't want to "come up." In order to do so, I had to "come down" and humble myself.

I thought being average was ok. I thought it was ok to settle and just be with any guy. But God wasn't playing with me! It was easy to be lukewarm, yet God kept spewing me out. I thought I could just stay silent and keep to myself. That was my definition of being humble. But that wasn't humility; that was bondage. As long as I was living and staying clear of people, I thought I was doing ok. But I wasn't.

Let's be real. I was a foolish bride. I was stupid to think I was content in the state I was in. I was a foolish virgin with no oil. I wasn't prepping, and I was running on empty. There wasn't any preparation in my moments of free time. And I certainly wasn't in God's will; I was in His way. I was in an idle, isolated state. Who was I kidding? There I was going through each day and watching them pass me by. I knew a decision had to be made, and soon. I had to choose to live on purpose. Having enough just wasn't enough. I wanted to have more than enough in my home, spirit, and life.

To have so much in storage that it overflows. Indeed, a virtuous woman wouldn't let her life and the light of who she was, become dry or dim. In fact, there is a constant willingness to be an overflowing vessel. A foolish bride will only have enough for today, but a wise bride will want to be a more than enough, overflowing woman.

So, I chose to let my light shine and be a vessel that has enough oil at home. I told myself that my setbacks would help me make a greater impact. I was determined to prosper, and because I was determined to flourish, I found my purpose.

Now, I'm in God's will, the one that was waiting for me all along. The one that He always intended for me to walk in. I'm living in purpose; I'm impacting lives; the light of Christ shines through me, and the Grace He has given me is overflowing in my life. Thanks to God's goodness, I can help others be filled with the richness of His glory and power.

I want you to know that no trial or obstacle can stop or block God's hand over your life. Situations don't dictate how we're seen. They are presented to test our faith, help us see ourselves, and see the Lord. I quickly learned that living is not about breathing easy and doing less. Living involves thinking of myself less and thinking about God more. In discovering my purpose, I learned that prayer was my key to find the Lord.

When I found Christ, I found the unlocked door that opened me to my destiny. I learned that my virtue came from being prepared and positioned for the Holy One. It was essential for me to understand the difference between living life my way and living in the full abundance that Christ wrought for me through the cross.

Jesus provided the example of what a virtuous woman can accomplish. His death and resurrection gives us hope and enables us to be the light that shines in the darkness.

So, no matter what you've done or where you feel you fall short, know that you can be virtuous because Jesus has given you life, and that, my friends, makes you new. He doesn't see you as a slave or a servant, He calls you His friends. We are the daughters, coheirs, and beneficiaries of the King of Kings.

Let's turn our focus to Queen Esther (see Esther 1-10). Did you know that her name means "star?" And she has a fantastic story, doesn't she? Esther was definitely a star. Because of her, we have an example of how God can cause the poor to rise with power. Esther is an example of a woman who never knew how needed she was. She was an average girl who was raised by her uncle.

Although Esther was poor, she had so much favor that she was wealthier and more beautiful than every other woman competing to be the next queen. While her place of origin was unknown, her virtuosity caused her to be ready and positioned at the right time to save her Jewish people from certain death. To put it simply, Esther was the undercover agent her people desperately needed.

This modest, humble woman had no choice but to be obedient, wise, and prayerful. Her favor brought her places that no other queen could get close to. Esther demonstrated how she had her man wrapped around her finger. She was so favored that her husband was willing to give her anything she wanted, including his kingdom. Talk about favor!

However, her husband was not her only assignment. She had to get in position to war for her people, or she would lose them forever. So, she got into a position of prayer; she fasted, she sought the Lord, and He redefined her. He made her shine. He turned a lower class girl into a queen.

He used her life as a conduit to save His chosen people because a Savior would soon come through them, the One who would save the world from the wages of sin. It was Esther's devotion to God that caused her to be a queen like no other. Her life of prayer enabled her to take necessary risks. She knew she couldn't forget her people.

She realized how much she was needed. Although she had started from the bottom, Esther became the epitome of what a virtuous woman is. She was on top. This is why her story is of the utmost importance. If it weren't for a virtuous Esther who took the place of a prideful Vashti, many lives would have been lost. But her obedience saved them. Pride couldn't do that.

Esther was redefined from her rags to her richness because she acted out in faith. She didn't let her position define her. Her faith and heart established her worth. Her reverence for God and trust in Him resulted in her becoming an example of selflessness. She was willing to sacrifice her life for her people. Now she, my dears, is a woman who knew who she was. Esther shined in glory, and she mattered. What a woman of virtue she was.

I'd like to reiterate that you can be virtuous, too. I cannot argue enough how necessary it is for you to be virtuous. You may be surprised to know that it also means to stand for something. As it is often said, if you don't stand for something, you'll fall for anything.

It is a rare commodity to be virtuous in a time where so many are lost. Living as light-bearers and glory-carriers of the Lord entails being a beacon of hope for those who have lost their sight for living. People aren't focused on the purity and glory that should resonate inside. Many are focused on repairing and renewing the outside. Which is why so many wear waist trainers, and even consider plastic surgery.

We're so geared on fixing the outer shell, but we don't want to perfect what's inside. However, a virtuous woman understands that the light of Christ has transformed her from the darkness of her past and has renewed her to the light of His glory. Because of the light of Christ, which dwells within her, this woman shines with favor, grace, and power. When you can accept that you're not just a woman, but God's daughter, the glory of the Lord doesn't just visit you, it stays upon you.

> *Arise, shine; for thy light is come, and the glory of the Lord is risen upon thee.*
>
> Is. 60:1 KJV

III

Changes & Challenges

In life, there are many challenges, and with them come inevitable change — curveballs of different changes and challenges we have no control over. Challenges help us change our perspective on life. The challenges we face, change us, and we learn how to run to them rather than from them.

Growing up, I had trouble accepting the constant changes that came with life. I hated the fact that I couldn't handle them. I went through many growing pains while I faced the various changes that came in my direction. I despised the process. I desired to have things in place and be in control. The Lord, however, had a different plan for me. I was ever so complacent and content with mediocrity, but God wanted to birth excellence out of me. I was ok with my routines and predictable outcomes. However, God wanted me to search and find Him. He wanted me to follow Him blindly. Without any clues, yet solely trusting in the

Holy Spirit to see my way through. But, knowing what to expect felt safe. Easy. I wanted a systematic and perfect life.

So, I built this Utopian, mundane life that made me feel good. I created this fantasy of having it all. Well, it did a number on me all right. He tore my walls down and wrecked my clichéd idea of what I thought my life should be. God crushed my definition of life and allowed me to see Him. The hand of God stripped me of selfish desires and directed me to His word and purpose.

I later learned that changes were necessary for my growth. Although some were a bit challenging, they all played a significant role in my journey. I grew up with many challenges. Some of my hardships were mostly psychological. I always struggled with accepting God's will for my life, struggling between choosing Him and staying lost. I struggled with insecurity and keeping relationships. I didn't think my life had any purpose. I had major self-esteem issues and always felt the need to switch my look.

To some, it was cool. But I knew I was looking for approval each time. I needed the instant gratification that a compliment provided. My constant changes had nothing to do with the money I had or a simple desire to try new things. It was rooted in my struggle to settle in who God called me to be for Him.

I struggled between accepting who God said I was and who I felt I should be. I kept trying to build and build until finally, I shut down. I didn't know that the challenges I had faced in the past were the ones that would perfect the character I needed. I had to accept that being a woman of God was a choice, and there was no way out of that. I just wanted to be, yet God wanted me to become. Become what He sees and come into the realization of who I am in Him.

It took a while to settle and stay submitted to the image I always was, but never wanted to see: "We can rejoice, too, when we run into problems and trials, for we know that they help us develop endurance. And endurance develops strength of character, and character strengthens our confident hope of salvation" (Rom. 5:3-4 NLT).

Change was a constant thing in my life, as it is for many of us. While it was something I initially rejected, through the word of God, I learned that it was inevitable and necessary. And so change became my daily, progressive process. Once I embraced the unavoidable, I was able to use the power I had to speak the change I wanted to see into my life and world (daily renewal).

In this life, you can't complain when change comes your way. For that is when God reveals more about yourself to you, and it is the result of these revelations that transform you. Without a doubt, change comes through life's experiences, but they come primarily through trials. The obstacles that you face are temporary tests that will help you train for the next level of your life. Change is the minor adjustment that flips your life in a different direction. As you adjust accordingly, you will see the results of the choices you've made and better understand the steps you will need to take.

Many of the turns you'll experience in your life may include a shift in your careers, goals, seasons, tastes, style, levels of spirituality, and even relationships. We may currently desire something, but God knows what we need. So, in His infinite wisdom, God comes in, and He shifts our gears. A strong wind of change comes and blows into our lives for a good, Godly purpose.

Let's say you wanted a job so bad that you prepared for it; prayed for it. Faithfully believed that you would get it, and then suddenly, God changes your perception of it. He reveals to you that you're settling and that He has a much bigger plan in the works for you. You waver and question whether you're hearing His voice, but deep down, you know the truth. You know when God is developing something greater in you, and so you walk away from it. That's the moment where the other offer comes. It's where you discover the better God had in mind for you all along. And you appreciate the Holy Spirit for protecting you from making a terrible permanent decision in a temporary situation. We may also feel that we're ready for an assignment God says we're not prepared for. He, then, works on us and teaches us a new lesson in the process.

My friends, change is good. It is strategically positioned by God to develop your character. Change is there to teach you about what you like and what you don't. With changes also come challenges. Challenges are difficult. They often feel like you're hitting a brick wall, or like you're running through an obstacle course. But it's a course that will upgrade your view of life.

When you hit a brick wall (such as a bad relationship), you're often severely hurt. But once you are acquainted with that pain, I'm sure you'll do whatever possible to avoid hitting that wall again. That's because you've learned something new, and there, my friends, is when your challenge receives a higher purpose: God wants others to benefit from your harrowing experience.

I can recall a time when I was madly in love with this guy. Well, at least I thought I was. I really wanted it to work. I prayed, I fasted, and I carried the relationship on my back. I was willing to make it work because I desperately wanted it to.

But this breezy fantasy of a relationship felt more like a ton of bricks. I was continually arguing, crying, fighting, and I was ignoring the signs. It just wasn't working. I loved the idea of a relationship with him, but the connection was detrimental to my life.

It caused me to be depressed, become doubtful, and left me with many regrets. It was clear that I was the one who chose to settle with this dead weight of a relationship following me around, and it wasn't pretty. Can you imagine carrying a dead corpse wherever you went? Imagine the stench of that connection everywhere. You can't conceal it. The disgusting aroma and weight of a dead thing are just too heavy and nauseating to carry around. I, eventually, had to cut ties with that guy and relieve myself from that dead-end love affair.

But, ending it wasn't easy. That brick wall had done a number on my face. The fleshly ties were plenty. Nonetheless, I was tired of trying to be superwoman. That relationship wasn't God's plan for me, so I let it go. The moment I did was the moment that I could breathe again: "Therefore, since we are surrounded by such a great cloud of witnesses, let us throw off everything that hinders and the sin that so easily entangles. And let us run with perseverance the race marked out for us" (Heb. 12:1 NIV).

Although your challenge was excruciating, it could help you help another avoid that brick wall. Because you'll remember how painful it was for you. The difficulties you face now become a lesson that you can teach another person. That is why we all need changes and challenges.

If everything were easy, then life would be predictable. Much can be predictable, but life shouldn't be one of them. It is just too amazing to be so: "Dear brothers and sisters, when troubles come your way, consider it an opportunity for great joy. For you know that when your faith is tested, your endurance has a chance to grow. So, let it grow, for when your endurance is fully developed, you will be perfect and complete, needing nothing" (Jas. 1:2-4 NLT).

Now let's take a closer look at Ruth's life (see Ruth 1-4). Ruth was struck with a burst of changes and challenges. She was a Moabite woman who married an Israelite, joined his family, and out of the blue, her husband dies. Unfortunate, isn't it? She had cleaved to this man, sojourned to find life with her man, build a life with him, hoped to have kids, and then he dies? Can you imagine such a turn of events? You get married and your husband up and dies at the prime of his life? "Difficult" doesn't begin to describe that kind of pain; of being a newlywed one day, and a widow the next. That was a change she didn't expect and a new challenge she had to accept.

When the time came for Ruth to part ways with her mother-in-law, Naomi, she decided to follow her. She took a route that was different than what was expected of her. In her faithfulness to be a caregiver and assistant to Naomi, she was inevitably compelled to deal with change. Her scenery had changed, her lifestyle had changed, and so had her environment. She went from being a Moabite idol-worshiping woman to learning from Naomi how to serve the true and living God.

Ruth's obedience to Naomi, her life of servitude and worship before God, led her to be blessed. It was her obedience that led her to the change in her life.

Her next level and shift came because of her choice to make a change. But I want to point out that she didn't know her future husband, Boaz, was tied to her next level. When the time for transformation had come, she fell right into place, at the opportune moment. And what a redefining moment it was! Ruth's status had shifted from that of a wife to a widow, to becoming a wife with substance! There was a strategic change that nursed the wounds of Ruth's life and accelerated her to blessings she never knew would come. This change in Ruth's life was good; it was divine. It had facilitated Ruth's defining hour. The winds of change had blown in her direction. She experienced a moment that defied the odds of the many challenges she faced, and she came out victorious.

As necessary as change is, I'm not saying that it should be so constant in your life that you are unstable. Too many changes and instability aren't biblical. The Bible clearly tells us that a double-minded man is unstable in all their ways (see Jas. 1:8).

While being open to change is good, too many changes without a purpose are not. I already explained how unstable I was when it came to changing my style.

That was because I didn't know who I was. Only Godly change is a good change. It is orchestrated to demonstrate the power and very hand of God moving on your behalf.

If you wanted to meet new people or find a job, you wouldn't go to the same location or follow the same patterns and expect a new outcome. As Albert Einstein said, "Insanity is doing the same thing over and over and expecting new results.

At this juncture of your life, you may feel that there are some challenges or significant changes that you have no control over. You're probably like, "Lord, what is going on?" I am sure Ruth was thinking the same thing when her husband died. Ruth trusted and leaned on a God she had barely known. While following Naomi's lead, Ruth took a risk and made a change. The winds of change blew on her behalf, and she was never the same.

My sister and dear friend, the wind of the Holy Spirit is blowing something new for you. If I were you, I would give God a shout and a scream, "Lord, I thank you for the changes and challenges You have allowed! I know You've got me covered!" Being lost and feeling confused is uncomfortable, but in fact, it can be beneficial. As King David said, "it was good that I was afflicted" (Ps. 119:71). All that you've faced was for your good! You had to go through. You had to lose. Some of the very things you lost has helped you gain a higher perspective in life.

Now, you're losing control, you're leaning less on worldly foundations and depending more on the King of Glory. Sometimes, feeling like you're at a standstill is good. You may not see where you are, but the place you currently are is in the will of God. So, you may as well REST there.

God has a way of calming your spirit so He can get your attention. Now you may not agree with me, because maybe this season of your life is very arduous. There may be a death, a divorce, or a dead-end road that you're facing. Perhaps you want immediate change, but you think that you're stuck. The truth is that you're not. You're just still.

Sometimes, God will calm the storms of your daily life to steer you back to the course of life He saw for you. This is a season of rescue for you. God is causing you to REST before He gives you your cue. Ruth had experienced a rest stop when she reached Naomi's hometown in Israel. God had stilled her after much turmoil, and that led to much reflection and preparation. At the right moment, Ruth took her cue, and her obedience caused her to be rescued.

Rescue is what happens when your life needs to be saved and redeemed; God wants to rescue you. A lifeguard is one that sits on a high chair observing the people who come to the beach or pool to swim. They save lives and perform CPR when needed.

When swimming, there are times that the current of the waters pulls you in deeper waters. Before you know it, you're further away from the shore you were once near, and you can't feel your feet on the ground. Or if you're in a pool, you can't swim because the water is too high. A swimmer who isn't adequately trained can drown in these circumstances. When a person is drowning and screaming for help, a lifeguard doesn't get in the water immediately. They wait until the individual is close to drowning.

By this time, the lifeguard is sure that the rescue is feasible. The unskilled swimmer is no longer a danger to the lifeguard or themselves, and the chances of both coming out alive are far greater. So, the lifeguard swims to the aide of the drowning swimmer.

A lifeguard can never sit and watch one die in the water. They must be wise enough to wait for the opportune moment. It is the same with the Lord and us. God is the lifeguard who is seated on His heavenly throne, watching intently on His chair as you get pulled in.

He sees that your hands are lifted in surrender and that you are gasping and screaming for help. God acknowledges that you're drowning in life's sea of problems. However, He waits until you are still. That is His cue to save you. When the issues of life overwhelm you, and you feel like you can't stay afloat, Jesus comes to your rescue. He is the lifeguard that helps you amid the changes and the challenges you face. He will always want to save you.

The wind of the Holy Spirit is blowing amazing things in your direction. Good godly change that will re-calibrate your entire existence for the glory of God. Don't you dare worry another minute! Surely, you are in the place where God wants you. Relax and realize that all that has happened and what's coming is all or-dained by God.

So, are you afraid of change now? Are you ready for the next challenge? My prayer is that you look at it squarely in the face and say, "Bring it on!" Because the next one could be the one that reroutes you to your promise, Ruth.

Know that you've got this, and you can do what-ever you set your mind to do. The Holy Spirit is with you and will lift you out of your dead-end situations and shift you to your next level. Remember that every season comes with a lesson and a test, and that, my dears, are why changes and challenges are necessary. Know that each trial will empower you to be healed, ex-perience wholeness, and lead you to a life of holiness.

IV

Healing, Wholeness & Holiness

Her pure approach to get healed and be changed led to her redefinition.

A redefined is a woman who is whole in every aspect of her being (her mind, body, spirit, and soul). She's fully healed and lacks nothing. There are no holes, voids, or empty cracks in a whole woman. She's not marred or broken, but she's altogether; fully intact. I want to focus on the importance of wholeness, the healing that enriches you to exude God's holiness, as well as shed light on some important key factors.

When Eve was created from the very rib of Adam, she was created whole. There were no errors; nothing was left out; Eve was complete. She was whole, and she was holy. How do I know this? Well, Eve was created by a divine, spiritual, celestial, holy God who made her perfectly. There was nothing impure about her. Even God acknowledged that she was good. Eve was filled with the likeness and the very breath of God. She was made with all the abilities and traits that a woman needed.

We all know that the devil is crafty. He beguiled her with his lying words to make her feel self-conscious. Eve fell for the trap, and we know how the story goes. The fall of man proceeded. Man lost their identity, their access to God, which means their ability to fellowship with Him was gone (see Gen. 3). And then entered Jesus (see Lk. 1-2).

What He did on the cross gave us new life. The enemy planned to steal our identity and value in the garden with the fall of man, but Jesus redeemed man through the cross. Today, women can be healed and whole, because of what Jesus gave us.

The cross gave our lives a future, destiny, and new meaning. The sacrifice of the cross caused us to be adopted and be called daughters, once again. Our identity, freedom, peace, mind, healing, and purpose was knitted together through the death and resurrection of Jesus Christ. It allowed us to have a chance to live and be renewed. Indeed, the cross took our infirmities and gave us our healing: "Who His own self bore our sins in His own body on the tree, that we, being dead to sins, should live unto righteousness: by whose stripes ye were healed" (1 Pet. 2:24 KJV).

The cross became the addition symbol that was also the solution to our problem. Humanity had a major problem. Sin separated man from God. The devil tried to divide and subtract us from the grace and meeting place of Eden. We were already seated, already made blameless. But, sin actualized our separation, parting us from our former nature to know God and be one with Him. It was always in our innate nature to be like God. When we were roped by Satan's trap, we fell into a corrupt life, and we immediately experienced a subtraction.

Jesus Christ, born of Mary, had to come and be the addition. He added Himself to our natural scenario to be the One who would bring back multiplication. Satan wanted our subtraction and separation because he was already extracted and removed; from heaven and from God's presence. He was jealous. Satan wanted man (whom God loved) to be on the outskirts too. So, he created a problem, but God had the solution. Where there was separation, Christ brought life again.

He was the addition that would make us whole again. We were equal when Satan came to subtract. So, God deducted Himself from man's presence. But He returned through Mary to be the additive that would make us whole, complete, and equal again. Wow. We were once singular and lost, but we aren't anymore. We are filled with the divinity of God. We are plural because the Father, Son, and Holy Ghost have made us whole.

As a result, we will always be able to multiply His love, goodness, and grace to those who need it. Jesus Christ gave us that power.

I've explained how the fall was dealt with through the cross, and how knowing Jesus Christ makes you whole. Jesus invades your life, and He gives it meaning again. He makes it worth living because He lives the plan and purpose of God in you. There's no way a woman can make Christ the Lord of her life and go on being empty.

If you feel empty, uncovered, or lacking, it is probably because something or someone has taken the Lord's place in your life. I don't know if you had a bad breakup or experienced a divorce. I don't know if you lost a loved one. Maybe you're broken or let down. I can only imagine how you might feel at this very moment. However, I know that if you're not ready to be healed, you will continue to go through life: hindered and inhibited. Have you ever considered that maybe you're not healed, and it could be stopping your progressive walk with Christ?

You need to know that healing is absolutely imperative. It's as progressive and instant as you allow it to be. Some hits in life hurt so bad. Every time you think about it, it's like you're struck with the pain all over again. Why re-live it? Why should you be the victim of an unbearable pain again and again?

Do you know that each time we recall the pain inflicted in our lives, that we bear the pain Christ already endured for us? "Surely, He hath borne our griefs, and carried our sorrows: yet we did esteem him stricken, smitten of God, and afflicted. But He was wounded for our transgressions,   He was bruised for our iniquities: the chastisement of our peace was upon Him; and with His stripes we are healed" (Is. 53:4-5 ASV).

"But, you don't know what I went through! You don't know what they said. You don't know how much I gave him or her. Oh, no! I can't forget that" you say. There are so many excuses we can rely on to rationalize and justify our pain. I know. I've been there. I've been in situations where I had to forgive people after they deceived me.

I remember when my best friend and I got into a terrible argument because she hurt me. She had successfully seduced a guy, my former boyfriend. What a blow that was! We worked at the same place and even served in the same ministry together. I mean, we were *best friends*. I felt so betrayed that I really struggled to forgive her. Every time I tried, I was reminded of what she had done. She practically *stole* him from me.

I thought the situation was too much to bear. God was continually convicting me to walk in love and forgive her. While I wasn't ready, I didn't want to go to hell, harboring hate for a girl that hurt me. So, I had to forgive her. There was no question about it. I chose to meet with the two, and I prayed for them. I released them from my spirit and cut myself from every tie of bitterness and resentment that was in my heart. Freedom never tasted sweeter.

I know that you've experienced hurt, and I know it's rather difficult to forget what it felt like to be abused, let down, disappointed, bewildered, and broken. It stung. Burned. I get it. You know what it felt like to cry, lose your job, your mate, or miscarry the child you longed to have.

My friends, you have faced loss and disappointments, and maybe you're still living through some, but you must let them go. In life, we will get hit with the pounces of life. Some knocks of life can be hard and can keep you down for a while. But if you'll allow Him. Jesus can take the pain when we are hit. He didn't come to just save your future. He came to help you live in your now.

This very moment is the time to let go, relieve yourself of the hurt, and place it in the hands of *Jehovah Shalom* (God, our Peace). Jesus came to heal your today, so you can live a better tomorrow. In your healing will come your peace.

Perhaps something or someone took your peace from you. But you can't proclaim peace without the faith to believe you can be healed. A life change or challenge affected your inner peace, and now internally, you are cluttered with darkness, shame, regret, sorrow, and maybe sin. Jesus wants to heal you right now. The word of God says, "He heals the brokenhearted and binds up their wounds" (Ps. 147:3 NIV).

God wants to heal your wounds and take your yoke upon Himself and make your burden light. I want you to believe you can be healed and accept your healing because in your faith to believe in your healing, then the peace will come.

> *And a woman was there who had been subject to bleeding for twelve years, but no one could heal her. She came up behind him and touched the edge of his cloak, and immediately her bleeding stopped. "Who touched me?" Jesus asked. When they all denied it, Peter said, "Master, the people are crowding and pressing against you." But Jesus said, "Someone touched me; I know that power has gone out from me." Then the woman, seeing that she could not go unnoticed, came trembling and fell at his feet. In the presence of all the people, she told why she had touched him and how she had been instantly healed. Then he said to her, "Daughter, your faith has healed you. Go in peace."*
>
> Lk. 8:43-48 KJV

It's important to note that after the woman with the issue of blood was healed, Jesus told her to go in peace. He wasn't telling her to go away, Jesus was telling her to go in the peace that was given. She was to walk and live in peace.

For 12 years, that woman had suffered. I'm pretty sure she had had enough. Can you imagine hemorrhaging that much for so long? I believe she experienced an epiphany where she recognized that her day of deliverance had finally come. Her day of redefinition had made a sudden arrival. That was the day she stopped nursing her infirmity, the day that she got over her suffering.

A significant change was about to challenge her faith. I believe her faith echoed through the chaos of crowds as Jesus was passing through, performing unbelievable miracles. This woman had one shot, one moment. The Jewish law of that time probably mandated that she be stoned for touching others in her state of uncleanness. She could've been trampled on and tossed aside in her attempt to reach the Master. Yet, she aggressively pursued Him, knowing in her heart that Jesus had what she needed.

Trying to get through, she was only close enough to touch his tallit (*tzvit*) — the hem of His garment. Jesus then paused and asked, "Who touched me? I felt virtue come out of me." Jesus asked who it was, and the woman suffering comes out and tells her story.

Another lesson we can learn from this story is that confession and honesty always bring healing, ladies. When we can be honest and bear our issues and sin with one another, it brings healing. The following scriptures confirm this:

> *Therefore, confess your sins to each other and pray for each other so that you may be healed. The prayer of a righteous man is powerful and effective.*
>
> Jas. 5:16 NIV

> *If we confess our sins, He is faithful and just and will forgive us our sins and purify us from all unrighteousness.*
>
> 1 Jn. 1:9 NIV

The bleeding woman of great faith was instantly healed from everything that touched her. Dipping into the source and power of the Holy One, she grabbed the true Healer. Formerly known as a suffering woman, she became a daughter. Jesus called her daughter. Her virtuous approach to get healed and be changed led to her redefinition. Only Jesus could have done that.

An exchange of healing came from a pure move of faith. Aggressive approaches result in acceleration. Great faith and sacrifice can cause us to move from being sick to being delivered. From being unclean to being clean. From being empty to being filled. From experiencing the old to being renewed.

We can be defined by infirmity. However, faith and pureness of heart can change our lives. They allow us to tap into the source and power of our God and make us healed, whole and holy.

Many of you may feel like you aren't healed or whole. But, you can be if you want to be. How bad do you want it? Like the woman with her twelve-year-issue, you're probably convinced that you've been this way for too long. And you may think that healing is impossible. You may have fallen short in your life. But, that does not disqualify you.

I also felt like I would never get over the pains of my past. But I overcame by the blood of the Lamb. It is crucial for you to know that you can overcome depression, your hurt, breakups, sin, and shame. Because what you thought was unfeasible is attainable through Christ Jesus, our Lord.

The woman with the issue of blood reached out and got a hold of her life when she caught the hem of His garment. She didn't just receive her healing, she was made whole. Jesus didn't heal her and leave her empty. He replaced the infirmity with His peace and power. She went to Him in peace, and her faith had made her whole. Although Sister Girl came bleeding, she definitely left with her healing.

Woman of virtue, I want you to know that you are healed! Christ already bore your infirmities. So, you are now whole because you've accepted Him as your Lord. You can now have peace because He dwells in you. His power and love will resonate and shine from within.

Because of His selfless sacrifice, healing, wholeness, and His righteousness is yours!

Man isn't holy by his own merit. Our righteousness is as filthy rags, but Jesus Christ has turned our rags turn into riches. He is now our righteousness! He has caused us to move from being a woman to being a child of God. The moment we acknowledge that we need a Savior, a Father, a Redeemer, and a Healer — that is what Christ becomes for us, and that is what His symbol of love gave on Calvary.

His example of love has thoroughly healed us and freed us from sin and infirmity. We've been given another chance and have been adopted by God. We are whole, we have a new identity, and now we can walk as co-heirs with Christ Jesus as we live in His holiness. With that said, my dear, I would like to pray for you.

Heavenly Father,

I present Your daughters right now. I pray that You would heal every broken area in their lives. Father God, in Your children's lives, I acknowledge and know that You are a Healer, a Redeemer, a Restorer, and a Great Physician. Lord, You're the best Counselor, Comforter, and Therapist there is. There are areas where they have fallen short, areas of pain, areas of hurt, areas of wounds that she no longer wants to bear. You said that You are our Healer. You bore our pain on the cross. So, in the name of Jesus, together, we let go of every hindrance, hurtful wound, or past pain that still lingers in their hearts. They want a better future because Your word tells us that we can have a life of abundance and peace.

So, Father God remove the pain, the letdowns, remove the wounds, heal every bleeding heart, every tormented mind, and broken promise that was given by man. Lord, restore the joy of Your salvation. Father God be Jehovah Shalom, our God of Peace. Be the peace that anchors us in times of pain. Lord, we replace every doubt with Your divine power, we exchange our burdens for beauty. We denounce the works of Satan, and we walk today, knowing that we are healed, whole. We can see You because Your holiness has allowed us to. Lord, I thank You for healing, thank You for dressing us in Your word, Your peace that surpasses all, understanding and your goodness (that we proclaim shall follow us all the days of our lives). We believe in You, almighty God. We grab ahold of Your garment of holiness that makes us whole today, and we won't let go. We love You and honor You forevermore.

In the Matchless Name of Jesus, We Pray,
Amen.

V

Refining for Redefinition

On this journey to redefinition, there's an essential and imperative process that we undergo. This process that I want to discuss is the refining process. Before there can be a proclamation of redefinition, there must be an absolute deviation from the flesh. The flesh has to become subject to the Holy Spirit. The Holy Spirit must have access to do a new work in the life of the believer.

here can't be redefinition until there's refining. "What is refining?" you ask. Well, it means to remove impurities or unwanted elements from *a substance.* Refinement is when the quality of an object is brought to its purest state. Many of us think we are fine just the way we are, but God wants to improve us.

That is especially true for those who want to be used by the Lord. If you're going to labor and serve in ministry or specific vocations for the Lord, you can't refuse the refining process.

Refinement is a requirement you can't bypass or ignore; for the Lord wants us to be refined, remolded, reshaped, and renewed. Refining is a never-ending, continual process that occurs in the lives of believers. Day in and day out, there is a constant need for improvement and correction. There is a consistent need for cleansing.

You've heard of refined oil, sugar, and metal. They are objects that are improved (refined) so that they are brought to their purest form. When these objects endure the process of refinement, their quality is transformed from their basic structure to their best form.

The purity and richness of refinement perfect its subjects (people or things). Although we can't be perfect, the process of purification is completed so that God can see the manifestation of His perfect will in us. When a person or thing is refined, it is to improve its quality — make it better than it was before. A refined position is a place where we are pressed, rebuffed, put in the fire, and purified repeatedly, as a goldsmith does to a piece of gold: "But He knows the way that I take; when He has tried me, I shall come out as gold" (Job 23:10 ESV).

Our heavenly Goldsmith keeps us in the fire until we are pure again. After melting us, He allows all impurities to lift so He can decide how He wants to use us. You see, God will refine us before He redefines us.

When God refines, it is so that we'll shine brighter than we ever have before. It's so that our quality will improve. So that others will no longer see us but see Christ in us. So that we can see Him, and He can see His image in us.

Refining occurs after much fire. The fire is there to burn out the fleshy desires, to kill our pride. To consume us and change us so that we no longer have selfish motives and sinful desires: "Behold, I have refined you, but not as silver; I have tried you in the furnace of affliction" (Is. 48:10 AMP).

There are seasons in your life where the pressure is applied at an all-time high. It feels unbearable. It feels horrible, but it is the pressure and fire of the Holy Spirit, consuming the very things that need to be evicted. The marring and impurities don't please the Lord, but it pleases Him to put us in the fire so that we will be pure as gold. Once you've been refined, you can now be redefined. The image of Christ radiates from the inside, out and there's a higher resolution that resonates. The higher definition of heaven's scope of who we are and what we are is defined through the high quality and high price that was paid. We are refined because we need to provide a proper presentation of who Christ is. With our participation comes preparation before major demonstration.

God will clean, rebuff, reprove, and remake us until not a spot of dirt remains. He desires to re-establish, reaffirm, and reposition us so that when others see us, they see what His definition is.

Refining is necessary; it is the prerequisite for your redefining moment. It is when heaven establishes its kingdom on earth, and the glory of God weighs in on the believer.

The righteousness of God that is imputed to us through the cross refines us. It causes us to be redefined. We are then no longer defined by sin or shamed by guilt, but we are infused with the power of the Lord's might and endowed with the glory of His grace. We no longer look around where we have fallen, but we look up to where we are destined.

Refinement is the removal of impurities so that we aren't infecting others with the infirmities of our sin and afflictions. Before Christ came, death was the only wage that sin allotted. But through His death and resurrection, Christ imputed grace and mercy, enabling us to fellowship with Him, even though we are unworthy.

Refinement exchanged the crimson stain and made us white as snow. The salvation call made us subject to redemption. Redemption received and rescued man—which brought us reconciliation. Reconciliation brought us renewal, and after much rinsing and repositioning, we no longer have rags but His righteousness—which gives us a right to stand for Him.

Refined believers are those whose light will pierce the darkness around them. They will shine the brightest, and they will be repairers of the breach where there has been a gap or a separation. Where disarray and malfunction have been set. Refiners will repair and be the ones to repel. Repelling against the swarming enemies. They will be catalysts of change. They will be the trailblazers who burn for the Lord.

Everywhere light-bearing believers go, their light will spare lives, aiding many to leave the path that leads to death and find life: "And I will put this third into the fire, and refine them as one refines silver, and test them as gold is tested. They will call upon My name, and I will answer them. I will say, "They are my people;" and they will say, "The Lord is my God'" (Zec. 13:9 ESV).

Simply put, refining is necessary. It is one of the steps that will lead you to a redefined life. You must go through a fiery trial; you must feel the pressure and the heat. There's no avoiding, dodging, or skipping this process. The more pressure a believer endures, the more power a believer will have.

Daniel 3 explains the story of Shadrach, Meshach, and Abednego, three devoted young men who were tested for their faith. King Nebuchadnezzar had made a decree. He ordered that they be thrown into a fiery furnace for not bowing to idol gods and embracing the ungodly lifestyle that was set before them.

When I think about this story, I see strong men of valor: men who felt pressure to conform but didn't. When the king decreed that he would kill them, Abednego decreed, "If you want to put us in the fire, our God whom we serve is able to deliver us from the fiery furnace and from your hand" (Dan. 3:17).

After the heat of the fire was magnified, and the guards who threw the three in were killed, something spectacular happened! King Nebuchadnezzar saw a fourth man, one who resembled the *Son of Man*. He immediately released the three men were not consumed or had a hair out of place. King Nebuchadnezzar had no choice but to honor and reverence the God of those three men.

In conclusion, what was supposed to kill Shadrach, Meshach, and Abednego made them even stronger and more respected. Although the heat of the fire was raised to the max, the men remained unharmed. That was because Jesus was in the fire with them.

Can I be honest with you? There were times in my personal life, where I thought I wasn't going to make it. I wanted to avoid the process of refining because it caused me to must bow, bend, be broken, and submit to the Lord. Although I didn't like the feeling, it was necessary to make me better. My faith became richer because of the refining I endured.

What made the three Hebrew boys exemplary was their stand for the Lord. Their foundation and assurance in their mighty God were sure. They were yielded and submitted sons. The point I'm trying to make is that a person who's willing to be seen or used by the Lord has to be connected to Him. To be an example or even a vessel that God can pour into, you must go through some pressure.

Even Jesus Christ went through pressing times. His defining moment was the pressing and the trial He went through in the garden of Gethsemane. That was the moment where He submitted to the will of God, which consisted that He die on the cross for you and me.

A refined moment is always a pressing, prying, painful moment where you must be crushed so that you can produce a greater product of yourself unto the Lord. You must be pressed; you must go through this way; you must submit to this process and say yes to the Lord. Every day is like a refining process. It involves choosing to lay your life down and saying, "God crush me till there's nothing left."

The thing is that your flesh must die. Your flesh

isn't going where your spirit is. Your flesh isn't saved. The flesh is our present trial, but that trial is only temporary. Indeed, we are spiritual beings having a human experience. We are celestial through the I AM that I AM.

We must submit to the Holy Spirit so that we can bear the resurrection and shine like JESUS. Every day we must bear the death of our Lord, so that we, too, can glory in His resurrected power (see 2 Cor. 4:10).

When you choose to withstand and go through the fiery trials that come your way, God will see you through. He won't let you pass through a fire that burns you, but He will be that fire that refines you. Our God is a consuming fire. He won't let you get burned, but He will buff you.

You can't call down any fire until you've been brought through the fire. You have to get to the point where daily you can emulate what Christ said in the garden: "Nevertheless not my will JESUS, but Yours be done" (Lk. 22:42).

God will make you stronger because a fiery trial isn't the end. It is the final touch before the presentation. Before your moment of resurrection, your elevation, your demonstration, or your next level. The Lord will allow you to go through a refining process so that you will shine brighter. You are His precious diamond in the earth.

Before a diamond even becomes a diamond, it's

actually a piece of charcoal. A diamond is a rare rock that is chiseled, precisely for a shiny presentation. A diamond actually endures refinement. It has to be buffed in extreme amounts of pressure and fire. Diamonds are formed because of the tension they experience deep within the earth.

It's a special jewel that's different from all the others. You're that unique jewel that God has to be particularly careful with. You're rare and cut precisely the way He wants. Because of the pressure, fire, grading, cutting, and calculations, there is a clarity and beauty that can be seen in you.

The Lord is not vicious for allowing you to endure refinement. His goal is to see His reflection in you. It's time to shine bright, beautiful one. Woman of God (and man of valor) reading this, maybe you're like the three Hebrew boys. You, too, are exceptional, hand-picked, set apart, and explicitly chosen to go through a fiery furnace so that you'll come out purer than before, stronger than before, and more powerful than ever before. Mal. 3:3-4 says it best:

And He shall sit as a refiner and purifier of silver: and He shall purify the sons of Levi, and purge them as gold and silver, that they may offer unto the Lord an offering in righteousness. Then shall the offering of Judah and Jerusalem be pleasant unto the Lord, as in the days of old.

A Redefined Woman

My prayer is that as a result of reading this book, you now understand who you are, and how imperative it is to be virtuous. Hopefully, you realize that change and challenges were placed in your life to position you for great lessons. I hope that you have chosen to receive the healing that has been made available through Christ Jesus.

Because of this, you now bear His righteousness, which merely means that you are now holy. More importantly, I pray that you have fully embraced what was discussed concerning the refining process. We learned that refining is the door that leads us to greater power. That redefinition becomes our final destination, thanks to the refinement we've endured. Because of all these things, our moment of redefinition can finally appear!

A great man once told me, "Rebecca, we must unlearn to learn again. We can't go to God with our 'glossaries,' but we must throw our books and 'glossaries' away and learn of Him."

In life, we have mastered the words taught to us. We have mastered our culture's words, music, traditions, and society. We have conquered the lessons and definitions given to us. We've accepted the stigmas and stereotypical standards they've set up. We ingested the words that scholars, poets, presidents passed on to us—definitions that we have held on to. But do they give us meaning?

Do the words line up with God's original word concerning you? What is your name? What does your name mean? For us to be redefined, we must first evaluate who we are now: *Who have I been? What am I connected to?*

Whenever you look at celebrities, you always find that most of them have a stage name and a birth name. Most stars with stage names reinvent their identity and personality by the stage name they're projecting.

When a celebrity changes their name, it is because they are building a brand. They're adding a new definition to their life. It's not that they don't like their original name, but it's probably that something in their lives has altered their way of thinking. I believe that everyone, whether it be through singleness, marriage, or even a change of environment, have defining moments that alter their perspective about who they are and what they do.

Similar to the words in a dictionary, every word spoken has a definition. Our names, our lives, when it 's viewed, has a distinctive print. A light and illuminating part of us is seen. It is this light in us that sets us apart. It is our DNA, our passion, our mind, our dreams, and vision that compels us to seek our God-given meaning.

When a person wakes up one day wanting to have a life with new meaning, it's literally the moment that purpose is bubbling forth. It is when the engine to the car of destiny pulls out of park and goes into drive. It is the *Kairos* moment where the Spirit of the Lord hovers over the depth of who you are and wants to create and manifest that which God has created and has longed to see you become!

In the beginning, when God created the world, more specifically, humanity, He took nothing and made it into something, causing creation to manifest from the dark and shine on in the light. We moved from being mere images and nameless things to being what God created and gave meaning to. Why would God create us in His image and say we're good and not allow us to know the significance behind who we are? Everything that God pulled from His mind and sculpted with His hands has a purpose. That purpose is not only to worship and glorify Him, but to be seen by Him, and through him (see Col. 1:16).

If you never thought there was meaning to what and who you are—believe me when I tell you—there are validity and purpose to your life. The same way God defined Adam and Eve's mission on Earth after they were created, He has done the same for you. You were designed to go through the stages of changes and lessons to be spiritually conscious and aware of who you are. All that we do, all that we say, isn't just seen, but it defines us to others, revealing to them who we indeed are.

When other people see us through God, they will know more than just our skin color. More than just our culture, more than just our career, talents, or gifts. People will know our God-given definition, and our name will bear meaning. There is more to you than just your name. You have a definition, and the redefined "you" is the "you" that has a new name and a new life.

Beloved, there is a definition! Although God sits on His heavenly throne, when He looks down at us, He sees us through high definition.

God's perspective is so magnified and so grand that nothing escapes it. He sees us with our beginning and end in mind. Most assuredly, only God can see things for what they truly are: viewing the natural as the supernatural wonder it is. It is always God's intention that our lives turn the attention of others to Him. So, in all the things that genetically, spiritually, and collectively make us, our lives should not just bring God glory, but it should be meaningful unto God. A life full of heaven's plan and purpose for you and me.

When people look at you, what do they see? Aside from your physical attributes, what is it about you that leaves an imprint or indelible mark of who you are? What about you makes an impact? A redefined believer is one that is defined by the word of God. The description, design, detail, and understanding of who we are and all that makes us whole are given by God. It is God's greatest desire to see His creation manifest all that He predestined for them to be.

Each of us has a time, a season, and a defining moment of becoming! For everything under heaven, there is a time. Assuredly, there is an appointed moment under heaven for us to pursue and to be. "Be what?" you ask. To be you. Be the "you" that God has called for you to become all along.

Jeremiah tells us that before we were formed in our mother's womb, our heavenly Father knew us. He knew a "you" that you haven't even met, known, or knew would ever exist. "How can that

be?" you ask. Well, my dears, Before the foundations of the world, God foresaw and predestined
who we would be. He knew it wouldn't be long before we have a burning desire to answer our own
questions: *Who am I? Why am I here?* God knew
you'd eventually make choices that lead to you becoming who you truly are.

Redefinition is about our divine distinction,
which makes us so beautifully different. It's about
understanding what makes you divinely you! It's
about embracing the new highs and accepting the
wisdom from your past lows. It's being proud of
who you were while remaining humble concerning
who you are today.

Redefinition is seeing yourself with the full
knowledge of your purpose by taking all you have
seen, felt, touched, heard, and living your truth.
Who we are isn't defined by culture or by religion.
Who we are is shaped and sculpted by God and the
revelation of His word to us. We are also formed by
the grace God has bestowed: allowing us to grasp
the notion that the scars of our past can help bring
out the best version of ourselves.

I've experienced a lot in my life. Writing this
book took me 8.5 years. It was many lessons learned
that helped shape my identity in God. I made so
many mistakes in the past, whether in my past

relationships or the poor decisions I made. I seriously felt that my choices interrupted destiny. Still, they were allowed to reach me and teach me passion, pursuit, and perspective through God. I know what it's like not to know who you are.

For this reason, I was so passionate to share with you how God sees you. I kept letting past relationships, and my culture define me, and that was very wrong on my part. I know what it's like to hate what I saw in the mirror because I thought that virtue came from external beauty. But it's not. It wasn't until I embraced my ugliness on the inside, that I was able to learn that a pure heart is what causes a woman to be radiant. That a praying woman who loves God first, herself second and others is, in fact, a beautiful, virtuous woman.

My pain taught me to be compassionate and live virtuously with others. And that, my friends, made me whole. I would never have been whole if I had held onto the hurt. I could never be healed living that way. Healing would have never come if I had held on to a futile, broken mindset.

My journey taught me that my name is significant! My name means that I am a connector. It means that I bring nations, people, and others together. It wasn't until I asked myself, "Who are you?" that I went on the discovery to find the answer in God. It took time. It took tears and, yes, many years for me to get it right. I couldn't help anyone until I first got myself together first.

My healing came through a complicated process, but I wouldn't change a thing. In my decision to write this book, I, too, had to journey towards healing to find hope, find inspiration, and reignite my faith in God. I couldn't touch anyone with my words until I let my wounds turn to scars. I couldn't do this process of healing, refinement, and redefinition until I could accept my old name and love embrace my new name in Christ.

While writing this book, I first let the words penetrate because I needed to believe them for myself. Beloved, redefinition involves choosing to accept newness. For me, it took trials and a constant refining process, but the outcome is that I know that who I am in Christ is great.

Redefinition is about a new you; a healed you. It's about being proud of the immature you by living in peace with what your past has taught you. It's about thanking God for the hurdles and the obstacles that came your way. It involves loving the curves, twists, and bumps of life and all the changes that shifted and helped enhance who you are. Changes and challenges that you didn't see coming did that for you. All that you and I have faced made us better.

Redefinition is about the metamorphosis that happens in you. It's when all that people defined you have shed, peeled off, and the true you on the inside shines through. Just like Christ's journey on Earth and the victory He won at Calvary, redefinition means a resurrected you! It's the authority you gain from a needed crucifixion.

After that, you become a "you" that has been tried and can walk in truth. A "you" that can testify about pain, the disappointments, and the shame and own it. It's like that cocoon that cracks open and reveals the butterfly that was forming inside. What everyone last remembered is not what they will see at your reveal! Redefinition involves seeing yourself through God's eyes and knowing His word and promises concerning you.

Because you've embraced very difficult refinement, and have endured the fire, you are now much softer. You're so much better than you ever were before. Redefinition brings you from your grave place to the place that grace has brought you. Discovering who we were predestined to be, by God, is a discovery of a spiritual exchange that leaves you full. It is a discovery that shocks you, shifts you, and when you're at the destined door of purpose, it seals you.

A redefined woman has been through obstacles, hurdles, circumstances, trials, and tests, but she has a message to tell. Through telling her story, she is pulled from the past and catapulted into the present. Her process of pain and refining has left her pure to be a redefined vessel. She's aware that her garments have been exchanged from ashes to beauty, from heaviness to praise. A redefined woman is a warrior, a daughter, sister, mother, aunt, grandmother, and woman of God. She roars through worship, wars in the spirit through prayer, and her praise unlocks the doors for purpose. A redefined woman is one who overcomes, and her story reveals how she survived. Her survival tactics and strategies are keys that unlock the next woman's door of destiny. She's a lioness and a lamb. She knows when to protect and when to project the proper traits for the assignment or task at hand.

A redefined woman wages good warfare and fights on her knees through prayer and supplication. She is one of a kind. Her signature, seal, and stance are significant. Her voice can't be replicated because it is original. When you hear her voice, you hear her heart.

She's a woman who is spiritually conscious, productively fruitful and ripe in her season. She is eternally minded and internally in tune: spirit, soul, and body. She is aware of her position and moves at a consistent pace with prayer, passion, and purpose. She is liberated, whole, and free from infiltration and manipulation. She is innovative. She is intelligent. She is unstoppable. She is unmovable. She is powerful.

A redefined woman is the queen of her home. She's blessed in her city. Blessed in her fields. Blessed when she comes, and also when she goes. She's always the head and not the tail. She's always above and not beneath. She never settles for less. She strives for the best because she serves under the best Father, best Teacher, best Lover, best Friend, Creator, and God.

A redefined woman is more than just the Proverbs 31 woman, she is all that and more. She's a P-31 woman, 2.0. She has been upgraded with grace, favor, and power. She isn't defined in doubt, in debt, or in darkness. But in her defining hour and moment, she is a light to her peers and loved ones.

She possesses greatness on the inside, and her presence and imprint demands respect, grants her authority, confidence, and serves notice to the enemy. She can't be moved, and she can't be hindered.

A redefined woman is who you are! You are whole, healed, holy, virtuous, renewed, reset, reinvented, relaunched, reclaimed, realigned, and, most importantly, regal. A redefined woman is who God says you are in Him, and nothing or no one can separate you from His love, His will, and His plan for your life.

Because you have embraced this redefinition, now when others see you, they'll see you as Christ does, as the new, redefined you; overflowing in anointing, grace, and God's sweet fragrance. You'll forever be associated with those things because You belong to Him, because He has set you apart and because He's on your side.

Today, I implore you to take hold of the tools you received from this book. I dare you to go forth and possess your promised land. Walk in confidence with your new identity in Christ Jesus. Walk in your new, branded seal from the shift that has brought you to this point. I believe that you, too, can say you are A redefined woman because pain isn't your name. Sorrow isn't your name. Death isn't your name. Low self-esteem. Witchcraft. Depression. Lust. Brokenness. Hurt. Rape. Molestation. Manipulation. Poverty. Jealousy. Pride. Envy. Anger. Being Fat. Ugly or anything that was spoken over you isn't your name!!

You are God's beloved. His prized possession. His jewel. His gem. His property. His creation, His beautiful masterpiece. The reinvented you has greatness on the inside, and now is the time for it to burst forth, singing the renown song that Diana Ross is known for "I'm Coming Out."

The paradigm shift of your divine destiny has shifted into gear. The glory of the former house is no longer at your address. Fresh dew is upon you. The fresh permeating scent of new wine is upon you, and now my sisters, you are ready. Go and live with your new, branded identity and personality. Your name is blessed, your name is whole, your name is changed. Your name is redefined.

Acknowledgments

A special thanks to:

God – Who is my everything. None of this could be done without His inspiration, gifting, and ability in and through me.

Mommy – The first thing you gave me was life, but the best foundation you've set for me was choosing Christ and living for Him.

Rachelle – We are forever unbreakable. No matter what.

Micaelle Previl – For editing my book and helping me to believe in myself enough to release this.